Celia

May 6, 1985

Blow Out the Wishbone

Blow Out the Wishbone

Carol Lynn Pearson

Bookcraft
Salt Lake City, Utah

Library of Congress Catalog Card Number: 84-73288
ISBN 0-88494-554-5

First Printing, 1985

Printed in the United States of America

All speakers in this book are the author's creation (partly), and any resemblance they bear to actual persons is absolutely natural.

Yesterday I gave Johnny his first wishbone. Holding one side of it, I said to him, "Make a wish, Johnny!"

"Okay," he said.

Then he took a deep breath, looked straight at the wishbone—and blew!

Do it any way you want, John. Blow out the candles, blow out the stars, blow out the wishbone. Just wish. Let your wonderful mind burst with all the possibilities of being. Fasten your eyes on the ones that set you on fire. And then wish—with all your breath, with all your heart, with all your soul.

Wishers and dreamers are the people who bring the future. They are not content with the world as it is. A brighter, better vision pulses in their imagination and they will it into reality.

The wish comes first, and then the work. Without work, the wish will dry up like an unwatered flower. But without the wish, work will go on and on, as hard and bare as flowerless ground.

Do both, my dear. But if ever you find yourself full of work and dry of dreams, run—do not walk—to the nearest wishbone, think up a great one—and blow!

The night before last I was putting Katy to bed after a very pleasant evening of being alone together here. She was being even more charming than usual, and I grabbed her and shook her and hugged her and said, "Oh, bless my little Katy!"

"Well," she responded. "That was a short prayer!"

That's one of the good things about prayer, Katy; it's very flexible. You can take it out anytime you want to and use it for any number of things.

You can take it out in the morning and let it cover you like a cloak, warming you and protecting you.

You can take it out at night and set it up like a scale, weighing what you have done against what you would like to do, and making plans to even things out.

You can take it out at mealtime and hang it like a sun over your table, encouraging the nourishment in the food and the drink.

You can take it out whenever something lovely happens and throw it like flowers in celebration.

You can take it out whenever sorrow comes and light it like a little fire and hold it between you and the cold.

You can take it out whenever you're lost and hold it in your palm like a compass. And when your hand stops shaking you can see the way home.

You can take it out when a friend needs cheer and blow it across the miles like a warm wind that lifts and heals.

Or you can take it out when your little girl is too darling for words and bounce it like a ball and catch it and laugh.

So bless you, Katy. Bless you, do you hear? Whenever a prayer is aimed your way, short or long, take it and be glad.

This afternoon Aaron and I were outside swinging.

10

Aaron: Mommy, I know why God sends babies to mothers.

Me: Why?

Aaron: So they won't fall out of the sky and land on the sidewalks and break their heads open.

No question about it, Aaron. Mothers make a wonderful landing spot. What a "splat" there would be without us! I spent nine full months preparing myself as a nice, safe, soft entry for you.

Mortality can be a shock, you know. Life is a hard, hard place. You will find things in this world that are harder even than sidewalks. You may break a few times. Just about everybody does. But there are places to crawl for comfort—soft places—family, friends, people who love you. And mothers.

Don't forget mothers. Even when you're too old to ask for my arms, don't forget mothers. We specialize in comfort, in softness, in warmth. We are halfway houses between heaven and earth. That's why God sends babies through us and to us in the first place—remember?

Not long ago I was making Aaron eat something he didn't want to eat. Johnny observed, "She's fattening you up, Aaron—just like she did to Hansel and Gretel."

How well I know, my dears, the fine line there is between being a mother and being a witch. Once in a while, as we go through our days together, I catch a look at myself in the mirror or hear the tone of my voice, and suddenly it is Halloween.

I'm sure I have sprouted warts, hat, broomstick and all before your very eyes on a number of occasions—when I made you write sentences instead of watching your favorite TV show because you forgot to write down your homework assignments; when I made you do more raking and cleaning and weeding than (you tell me) your friends ever did; when I made you wash windows at the neighbor's after having done unintentional damage there; when I made you stay in for two whole days for using language that needed a trip through the laundry; when I sent you from the table to eat in the garage because you karated the bread; when I made you return to your friend the bicycle accessories he had stolen from a bike at school and sold to you, and insisted he right the wrong.

We witches are out to do our magic, it's true. But I am not the Wicked Witch of the West, and I am not out to turn you into a toad. I am the Good Witch of the Sky, and I am out to turn you into the very best person you can possibly be. Or help a little, at least.

Recently Emily said to her daddy, "We love Jesus."

"Yes, we do," he replied. "And do you know what that means?"

Emily smiled. "That means we don't hit him or push him."

Correct, Emily. Correct. And it sounds easy. But do you know how *hard* it really is?

You might think, as you look around the playground, that Jesus is not there. There's Tina and Mark and Eric and Susan. But Jesus is nowhere to be seen.

Wrong.

Jesus put it this way: "Inasmuch as ye have done it unto one of the least of these . . . ye have done it unto me." So when you're hitting Tina, you're hitting Jesus. And when you're pushing Eric, you're pushing Jesus.

I don't understand it either, but there is a magical way in which we are all one, and the wounds we give to one are felt by all, especially by Christ. And the kindnesses we do for one are felt by all, especially by Christ. The playground violence, the domestic violence, the national and international violence have dealt blows to him that we cannot even imagine.

So when you're lined up for the slippery slide and somebody pushes his way in front of you—when you're in a classroom and the teacher embarrasses you—when you're at home and your brother calls you ugly—when you're at work and the boss takes credit for a job you did—when the neighbor's dog gets into your garbage for the third day in a row—look around at who else is there.

Jesus is there. And if we love Jesus, that means we don't hit him or push him.

This morning Aaron followed me into the bathroom where I was putting up my hair. He held up a piece of cracker he was eating and said thoughtfully, "Mommy—do you think this looks like a man with his hands in his pockets?"

I examined it and said, "Well, yes, it sort of does. What do you think?"

Aaron took it back and looked at it. "Nope," he said.

Y ou caught me that time, Aaron. And I've been caught before. And I'll probably be caught again. I'm too agreeable sometimes—agreeing with things I might not really believe—making myself see things that other people see even when I don't really see them, even when they're not really there.

Trusting your own eyesight, Aaron, while respecting other people's views is pretty tricky. And terribly important. There are lots of salesmen out there, wanting to sell you lots of things—cars, pots and pans, insurance policies, ideas, lifestyles, philosophies, beliefs. Watch out. If you listen long enough to somebody else, you can find yourself trusting what he *says* instead of what you *see*.

Just keep your eye on the cracker. And don't let anybody tell you something that doesn't fit with what you see —about life, about God, about yourself, about how to behave, about what's important.

It's good to be agreeable, Aaron. But don't be too agreeable. Don't violate your own vision. The cracker is right in front of you. Listen to what others say. And then be true to what you see.

Last night at the dinner table, Katy was taking a second helping of Chinese chicken and vegetables. She was picking out only the pieces of chicken and we told her to take some vegetables too.

"No," she said. "I only want the chicken." And she continued to search out the pieces.

Finally Johnny, in exasperation, said, "Katy—I don't care what Mister Rogers says—you're not that special!"

ow do we walk that fine line between being special and not *that* special? There is something in us that needs to feel unique and valuable and in some ways just a touch above the crowd. How can we regard ourselves highly, but not so highly that we think we should get all the chicken?

How can we love our country and salute its flag and sing its rousing songs and avoid the temptation to put into concentration camps and gas chambers those whose physical makeup or nationality or race is different from ours? Or make up unkind jokes about them? No one is that special.

How can we love our religion and yet refrain from judging others who choose not to follow that religion? Even today people are hanging others who insist on worshipping God differently. No one is that special.

How can we be proud of the fruits of our work and yet compassionate toward those less materially blessed? At this moment there are women leisurely deciding which diamond to put on today and men deciding which of ten cars to use, while another woman comforts a child in the last stages of starvation and another man cries in the night because he can't support his family. Many rich people try hard to share the chicken. Others, seemingly without a thought, take all the good pieces for themselves. No one is that special.

Keep reminding us, John. But do it humbly. You're a good observer. You're very special. But—well, you know.

This morning I was hugging and kissing Katy (my fourth child), and I said to her, "Oh, Katy—how did I get you? I must have won the contest and you were first prize!"

Katy laughed. "Oh, no, Mom. I was fourth prize!"

Fourth prize? *You?* Absurd!

Do you know what, Katy? We human beings have got ourselves into such trouble since we learned how to count. Does there always have to be a first and a last, a best and a worst, or even a better than?

Is first best? You put on your socks first and your shoes second. Does that mean your socks are better than your shoes? The Bible says that Adam was created first and Eve second, and lots of people think that makes man better than woman. But the horse was made before Adam. Does that make the horse better than man? You see, it gets very tricky. We have made up our games with our numbers and our prizes and we give out our ribbons and sometimes it helps and sometimes it messes us up.

Go ahead and do your math papers, my dear. But sometimes let's forget we ever learned how to count. We're not numbered. We just *are*. And you know what we're going to find out one day? We're all *first prize!*

Last week as we were driving to school, this conversation occurred:

Johnny: Don't pick up anybody this morning, Mom.

Me: Why?

Johnny: 'Cause you always start singing and they giggle and it embarrasses me.

Me: Well, there's no one but us here now, so may I sing?

Johnny: Okay, but make sure all the windows are closed.

Now really!

Do you have any idea, John, how desperately the world needs a little more singing—even from voices like mine that don't sound at all like they came from the same species that produced Sills and Streisand and Pavarotti?

Some wise person observed that most people die with their music still in them. I believe that too many people sing with their windows shut. There are enough sad sounds out there—sounds of anger, sorrow, frustration, despair. Whenever happiness happens, don't keep it quiet. Let it burst into whatever is most handy—a laugh, a joke, a song.

Watch out, John. I'm probably going to continue to embarrass you in the car by bursting into song without warning. And what's more, I'm going to invite everyone I know to open all their windows and sing. Real loud.

Recently at the nursery at church Emily had a very large girl for her teacher. She came home and said, "Mommy, my teacher is fat."

"Well, I hope you didn't tell her that," I said.

"No, I didn't," said Emily.

I then gave her a little discussion on not mentioning things to people that would make them feel bad.

Next week after nursery, Emily said, "Mommy, I told my teacher she was fat."

"Oh, Emily!" I said in dismay.

"But it's all right," she hastily added. "She already knew!"

Knowing isn't always the answer, is it? I *know* plenty of things that don't necessarily benefit me.

I know, for instance, that if I don't exercise my stomach muscles, they will get even more flabby than they already are. But sometimes that knowledge is not enough to motivate me when it's late at night and I fall into bed instead of doing my sit-ups.

And I know that getting into a contest of wills with Aaron over a piano assignment is not going to work, because when we lock horns *nobody* wins. But that doesn't always stop me from letting myself get pushed into it. And then being furious that I did.

We know that the planet is in danger. We know that our technological advancements far outstrip our spiritual advancements. We know we have the capacity to destroy ourselves. But that knowledge alone won't save us. Knowledge is easy to come by. Wisdom is not.

Go ahead and inform the world what's wrong, Emily. Announce to us our personal and our collective flaws. But that might not take care of all the problems.

Chances are we already know.

Recently Aaron was telling me a story I couldn't make any sense out of.

"Tell me again, Aaron," I said. "I don't understand."

He went through it again and I still couldn't get it.

"Try it one more time," I said.

"Oh, Mom," he sighed. "I'll explain it again when you're a little older."

O h, Aaron, I keep waiting for understanding. Really I do. And it comes, bit by bit, year by year.

I thought it was easy: first grade, then second; high school, then college; then you're a big person and you can figure out anything. You might have to go over it a time or two, but you can figure it out.

But life does not seem to respect that easy order. It stands right in front of me and tells me things, absurd things, things that I absolutely cannot understand, however hard I listen, however many times the message is repeated.

"There is war," says life. "People pick up guns and bombs and kill each other."

"What?" I exclaim in horror.

The message is repeated, making no more sense than before.

"A child is run over by a bus," says life. "The Mafia makes billions. The economy goes crazy and people are turned out of their homes."

I move closer to see if I heard right. "I beg your pardon?"

The message is repeated. Over and over. I shake my head.

Will I understand when I'm a little older? Will life articulate it a little more clearly and will I say, "Oh, I get it now"? Or will I go out of this world shaking my head, hoping that eternity will explain what life cannot. Probably the latter. I have to believe there is some final sense to all this, that somewhere, sometime, someone can explain it adequately. In the meantime I'll just listen the best I can and wait, wait until I'm a little older.

Just this minute I was hugging Johnny and asking him how he did in school today.

"Terrific," he said.

"How about math?"

"Terrific."

"Did you get them all right? Were you speedy?"

"Yes."

"Quick—what's eleven take away seven?"

Johnny thought a moment, then replied, "That's the only one I need to work on."

Keeps you humble, doesn't it, John? Just when you think you've got your act together, you find out there's something you still need to work on. Nature or life or God seems to give us the *exact* problem we don't have the answer to.

You're born and by two or three you've got it all figured out. Then life throws something new at you, maybe a baby sister, and suddenly *sharing* is the one you need to work on.

You sail through elementary school and hit junior high and suddenly there's a whole page of fractions, and it'll probably take you a whole hour and you'd much rather be out on your skateboard. So *discipline* is the one you need to work on.

You grow up and graduate and get a job and get married, and you're deliriously happy. But your wife doesn't like to cook what you like to eat, and she has a different opinion on the movie you just saw, and her idea of a clean house is different from yours. And suddenly *compromise* is the one you need to work on.

Then you have children and you know they will grow up to be perfect. But they don't pick up after themselves and they embarrass you in front of your friends and you have to tell them more than once to wash their hands for dinner. And you find that *patience* is the one you need to work on. And *faith*. And *acceptance*. And *self-control*.

Does anybody ever get their act absolutely and totally together? If so, life gives us death, and we move along to whatever thing there is over there that we need to work on.

Today I was insisting that Emily go to her ballet class when she wanted to stay home. She was in tears. Johnny broke in—

"Mama, don't you have any respect for a little girl who feels her feelings and you don't feel her feelings?"

Ah, yes. Nobody really feels another person's feelings, do they? Feelings are private, like blood and breath. They're *yours*—and try as I may I can't make them mine.

But the trying is important. Empathy, it's called, the attempt to get inside of someone else's mind and heart, and experience what they're experiencing. Or at least understand it. The Indians gave us the phrase, "Don't judge a man until you've walked a mile in his mocassins." We can try. We can put aside how we think it ought to be done, or how we think somebody ought to behave, or how we think they ought to feel—and try to enter into their experience, their own private world, share what has happened to them and what it is doing to them inside.

That's what actors have to do, you know. They have to take a character and get right inside, become that person so fully that they really do feel their feelings. And the audience peeking in knows those feelings are being felt, deeply felt.

I've done that on the stage. In college I did everything I could to put myself in the mind and the heart of Joan of Arc. And it worked. I felt her feelings. I cried her tears. It was a wonderful thing.

I guess I should try it more often, huh? Even with my children. Thanks for reminding me. I'll try to remember that even when the feelings belong to somebody else, if I can just be still and try—maybe I can feel them too.

As we were driving home from rehearsal tonight, this wonderful exchange took place:

Aaron: Oh, Mom—we don't have school on Monday. It's Veterinarians' Day.

John (with a laugh): No, Aaron! Don't you know what a veterinarian is? It's a person who doesn't eat meat!

It was funny when you did it, Johnny. But it's not funny when most of us correct one wrong with another. Sometimes it's pretty sad.

It was sad decades ago in Russia when the people right-fully decided there was a better life for them than the tyrannous reign of the Czars. But do you know what they came up with to replace it? A communistic government that forces upon them the severest restrictions on personal liberty. Is it a step forward?

And it was sad centuries ago when the Christian crusaders set out to right the wrong of religious oppression. How many people were slaughtered as a supposed service to God? Is murder ever a true correction?

It is sad in our own time when the wrong of sexual ignorance is being replaced by the wrong of sexual license. We used to have people terrified of the pleasures of their own bodies. But now we have a decline in lasting romantic love, an epidemic of venereal disease and unwanted pregnancies, and increasing psychological scars from the alienation of sex and commitment. If Victorian prudery was not the correct answer, is casual sex any better?

Do you know what I read in the paper this morning? It made me angry. For the first time, lung cancer outranks breast cancer as a cause of death among women, due to the rise in use of tobacco. For centuries—dark, sad centuries—women were not given the freedom and validation that men were. That was a wrong answer. And now we're happily figuring out a better statement. Some of it is better, but some of it is not. If being denied men's privileges was wrong, is the answer to adopt men's stupidities?

Raise your hand to correct a wrong every time you see one, Johnny. But make sure that when you do, you've got something better to offer.

We've been in our new home for three months now. A couple of weeks after we moved in, I was out on the balcony of my bedroom drying my hair in the sun. Katy, now three, came out and locked the door behind her. The other children were at school, and all the neighbors seemed to be at work. I called and called, "Can anybody hear me?"

At last a face appeared in some trees not too far away, and I gave a young man instructions on how to come and rescue us.

I gave Katy a strong lecture on not locking doors, especially as this came soon upon our having to call the fire department to get her out of my friend Jan's bathroom.

Katy now says regularly, "I don't lock doors anymore!"

But you will be tempted, Katy. We are all of us tempted to lock doors. And the doors that no one can open from the other side are the scariest of all.

Why do we lock ourselves in? For security? Protection? We seem most comfortable in a small, closed space that refuses entrance to the rest of the world. And if we stay inside long enough, we forget there is a rest of the world.

There are too many locked doors, I think. Too many countries have gone inside and locked their doors, and people as well as political philosophies cannot come and go freely. Too many religions have locked their doors, and enlightening exchange is not possible. Too many minds have locked their doors, and new ideas cannot come in no matter how hard they knock.

Shelter is good. Structure is needed. But watch out for doors, Katy. They're for moving through. When they're locked they become walls. And the world has too many walls as it is.

Our scripture for the week is "Peace, be still." Johnny read us the story on Sunday and we've talked about calming the storms inside of us.

Yesterday I let the children watch "The Miracle Worker" on television, the story of Helen Keller and her teacher.

At the part where Helen is still a wild animal, raging at her teacher, Aaron— completely involved—called out to her, "Peace, be still, Helen. Peace, be still!"

What a wonderful word, *peace*! It brings images of a calm lake in the mountains at sunset—of rifles laid down after a truce—of a clear, clean conscience—of a lullaby sung to a nodding child—of the smile on the face of a very old man rocking in the sun.

Let peace be your motto, Aaron. And your guide. I have found that peace is the best guide of all. It knows the terrain better than an Indian scout in the unexplored West. Follow it.

Whenever decisions have to be made, go with the one that is marked by peace. If a particular course leaves you in turmoil and unrest, you will know that is not a right course for you. But if that course, or the thinking about it, brings a feeling of peace, that is a sure sign that it is good. Not a resigned giving up—not an "Oh, well, this seems the easiest way." Sometimes the best course is one of difficulty, even of some danger, of uncertain outcome. But if the decision to follow it lets you sleep well at night—if you know that having followed it you could slip into death with a large measure of peace in your heart—go for it.

And when the unavoidable storms of life come, let peace find a permanent home within you, a place at your center from which it can radiate like a little sun.

You can then handle the weather. When the waves start tossing, you know the words. And you know they work. "Peace—be still."

Saturday Emily and I drove to the library together. Coming home the radio was on and the news reported that a twelve-year-old girl suffered some broken vertebrae in an accident. Emily looked at me puzzled and asked, "Why did she just suffer? Why didn't she go to the hospital?"

I laughed. Of course she went to the hospital. When one breaks a bone one heads straight for the hospital.

But I have discovered that when a break cannot be seen in an X-ray—when the hurt is in the heart or in the head—one sometimes does just sit around and suffer.

There are sadnesses in the human condition that we can do little about. Some pain is an inevitable companion of growth. And it must be endured, even welcomed. Without rain nothing grows and greens.

But when the pain does not go away—when the rain continues to fall and fall—should we not have enough sense to come in out of the rain—to *do* something about the pain?

I have seen people stay out in the rain until they drown. I have seen people hold pain close against their hearts and exclaim, "Oh, another blessing from the Lord!" They feel if they can just endure to the end they will be blessed, that a state of pain must be the natural state of mortality.

I believe that wholeness and health and contentment are the natural state of mortality and that chronic pain is a symptom that something is wrong and ought to be righted —something in our lives, our relationships, our work, our beliefs, our view of ourselves.

Do you know what happens, Emily, when one does just sit around and suffer? Unattended emotional or spiritual pain moves into the body and manifests in physical illness. We can be eaten alive by pain that we refuse to treat. And then well might we shake our heads and ask, "Why? Why did she just *suffer*?"

While I was at a meeting the other day, Johnny went to stay at the Williamses'. The house was rather disheveled—the ironing board was out, and so on.

Johnny looked around and said, "Do you have any children?"

"No," she replied.

"Then who made this mess?" he demanded.

Surprise, John! Big people make messes too. In fact, kids make little messes, and grown-ups make big ones.

One of these days, when you're tall enough really to see the world—when you can see the prisons packed and overflowing—the nuclear armaments poised for a final flight—the scars on the ancient face of Mother Nature—the hungry and the wasteful living side by side—the borders, physical and spiritual, that divide people—you will look around in disbelief and say, "Who made this mess?"

Well, we did. I did. And the people that came before me. And the people that came before them. And we were all little children who had to pick up after the grown-ups. There's the injustice. Big people make the messes and pass them on as an inheritance.

But there's no point in trying to fix the blame. You're young, John. You've got energy. You've got vision. The only solution is for each of us to start picking up fast. Never mind who made the mess. If each of us leaves the world a little better than we found it—we might see the mess begin to disappear before our very eyes.

We had an overnight adventure with the Andersens night before last. On the way home the children each had a balloon I had given them. Emily's popped and she burst into tears.

Johnny responded, "Good thing it wasn't mine!"

ine." A good word. A useful word. Also a deceptive word. Is anything just "mine"? Is anything just "yours"? Is there really an absolute "me" and an absolute "you"?

We seem to be tucked away nicely and privately in our own separate skin, a warm little wall that protects us from everyone's problems but our own. And from inside that effective border we can peer out and say, "Oh—children are starving in Bangladesh. Good thing they're not mine!" Or we can say, "A house burned down just up the street this morning. Good thing it wasn't mine!"

But our borders are getting less and less clear. We can't say, "The air sure is getting polluted these days. Good thing it isn't mine!" Or, "The government certainly seems to have a lot of corruption in it. Good thing it isn't mine!" And it will unfortunately not be possible ever to say, "Nuclear war destroyed a whole civilization. Good thing it wasn't mine!"

And there are other ways, too, that our singular possessive pronoun does not hold up. We are discovering that spiritually and psychically every living thing has connections beyond anything we've ever dreamed. Trees amazingly send messages to one another of approaching disease. Monkeys on one island suddenly demonstrate behavior learned by monkeys on another island. Human beings have photographable auras that change in response to the emotions that are received from and sent to others. We are all of us related by billions of unseen threads. So, finally, whatever enriches one enriches all, and whatever impoverishes one impoverishes all.

In some magical way that we will one day understand—wherever flowers are given or balloons are popped, they are mine.

The children and I all flew down to San Diego last week. As we got on the plane the only seats that were together were in a row that faced the opposite direction from all the other seats. After we had been up in the air a little while, Katy looked out of the window, then looked at me with a touch of horror and said—

"Mom, why is this plane going backwards?"

Oh, Katy, I cannot tell you how many times in the next years you are going to look around and think that the whole world is going past you backwards—that the life that carries you is headed in the wrong direction.

You will look out of the window, and through the clouds and the storms you will see things that will horrify you—disappointment, pain, illness, heartbreak, death—and you will say to yourself that the plane and the pilot have really done you dirt. Everything is backwards!

Well, before you bail out, my dear, try something else. Change seats. Get a different position for a different point of view. The sights out of the window may not change much, but they might make a bit more sense. The pilot has things under control. Life is headed in the right direction. Just fasten your seat belt, relax, and enjoy the flight.

Before our trip I had bought John some great sneakers at the thrift store for two dollars. While we were gone I asked him if he had brought them.

"No," he said.

"Did you lose them?" I asked.

"Well," he said. "What can you expect from cheap shoes? You pay two dollars for shoes— you lose them!"

You get what you pay for, is that it?

Money is maddening, isn't it, John? It gives us such an easy way to judge the value of things. The more money a thing costs, the more valuable it is. And if we're really lucky, all our things cost lots of money. Like the little rich kid who told his parents, after he came home from his first day at kindergarten, "We learned the pledge of allegiance today. But we only got so far as the place where you put your hand over the alligator."

He may be surprised one day to learn that there are shirts that don't have alligators on them. And he may be more surprised to learn (if he's lucky enough to learn it) that it really doesn't matter much.

Like the woman who held up a dress on sale and sniffed, "Hmm—forty dollars? I wouldn't even buy it if it was *eighty* dollars!"—we finally come to understand that price tags really don't mean much.

However, your investment theory, I have learned, holds up when it comes to the intangible things. If you invest two dollars' worth of yourself in a relationship—you lose it. If you invest two dollars worth of yourself in an education or in a job—you lose it. If you invest two dollars worth of yourself in a talent you'd like to develop—you lose it. These things take all the resources you've got.

I will never give up looking for bargains, John, even if the time comes when I don't have to. And don't you dare be too proud to wear a good bargain if you find one. But in the really important things of life, the things that money can't buy, don't settle for the two-dollar bargain. That's where you really do get what you pay for.

Emily continues on her own witty way. This morning she came to breakfast, looked at her scrambled eggs, whole wheat muffin, and orange sections, and said, "But—but I ordered a jelly roll and four doughnuts!"

48

rankly, Emily, I don't know anybody in this world who has gotten exactly what they ordered. And it's probably a good thing too. What a soft lot we would be if we all had a diet of jelly rolls and doughnuts—or whatever else is our favorite indulgence. And what a *really* soft lot we would be if we all could lie on the beaches all day and party all night.

Everything we want is on the menu—perfect health, the undying love of someone we adore, professional success, wealth, physical beauty, etc., etc. And if we're fortunate, we'll get some of those things.

But every once in a while we will look down at what's served up on that cosmic tray—down at the cancer surgery, or the six months of unemployment, or the broken heart from a love that went wrong, or a house washed away by flood, or the death of a dear one, or a child who scars himself by destructive behavior—we will look down at those things or other sorrows and then glance up at the great kitchen in the sky and exclaim, "But—but I didn't order this! I ordered health and wealth and happiness! The waiter made a mistake!"

But I don't think exchanges will be made. They never have been for me. I have come to believe, however, that if we take it well—if we try to understand it and learn from it and grow through it, if we let it strengthen us—we can perhaps come to see that maybe, just maybe, we are being better nourished than if we'd been given the jelly roll and doughnuts.

Recently when Katy and I were in the car she said, "Let's sing a song from 'Annie.'"

"Okay," I said. "Shall we sing 'Tomorrow'?"

"No," she said. "Let's sing now."

It's wonderful to have tomorrow, isn't it? Except that sometimes we let it take the place of today. Oh, do it *now*, whatever it is. Whether it's singing or writing a letter to a friend who needs to hear from you, or making that phone call that would open up some new opportunity, or starting that exercise program or diet, or beginning work on the paper that isn't due for two weeks, or telling someone that you love how important they are to you, or stopping to watch the sun set or the sun rise.

Professor Harold Hill in "The Music Man" said something like this: "If you put off everything until tomorrow, all you have left is a lot of empty yesterdays." The word is procrastination. It means intending to do something, but not right now. Sometime, but not now. I know people who just can't manage to get around to things, even things that they really want to do. It saddens me. They are piling up such a lot of empty yesterdays.

When you're young, it's easy to feel immortal. Well, we are, in a sense, but we are also mortal. We are all going to die and move on to whatever next step there is. Finally we will run out of tomorrows.

Don't count on anything but today. "Tomorrow" is a great song. But if you want to sing it, sing it *now*!

The other day, after Aaron had been playing outside for a long time, he came in and I said, "Well, Aaron—where have you been all my life?"

He answered, "In heaven, mostly."

I'm thirty-two years ahead of you, Aaron.
Or is it thirty-two years behind you?

I'm older than you. But you're newer than me. Age is confusing.

A very wise, elderly woman friend of mine once told me, "An adult is a badly deteriorated child." Being an adult, I could laugh that off, except that it's uncomfortably close to what another person said a very long time ago. "Except ye . . . become as little children, ye shall not enter into the kingdom of heaven."

I study the faces on the playground and the faces on the five o'clock commuter train. The faces on the playground smile a lot, laugh a lot, follow a bug in wide-eyed fascination, cry for a minute but then smile again. There is generally a look of trust and of hope. The faces on the train frown a lot, close their eyes in an exhausted stupor, turn away when a blind man comes through, or perhaps bury themselves in the pages of the stock exchange. And there is often a look of cynicism, of anxiety, or disappointment.

I probably shouldn't even be telling you this, Aaron. Don't get too uppity on me. Just now I have to be in charge. After all, I am thirty-two years ahead of you.

Or is it behind you?

I think so too, Katy. I really do. And I say that after having seen lots of storms.

It's funny. When we're in the middle of one of the storms of life, it's hard to remember how the sky looked before the storm began. It seems that the gray has been with us forever. Oh, we remember what blue looks like, but it's all very foreign now. We remember that there was a time when we were happy, but we can't remember quite how happiness feels.

And certainly in the middle of the storm it's difficult to believe that it's ever going to end. It seems that the rain is going to go on and on and on forever. Will happiness and peace ever come again? The storm says no.

But then—there is the rainbow! It was not gone forever, as the storm told us it was. The darkness lied. There are all the bright colors of sense and joy and success and love and contentment.

I don't trust the storms much any more. They're here for a reason, but I don't believe everything they say.

I listen to rainbows, though. I think you're right, Katy. Rainbows are the truth.

Last week I came out of my office and was very upset to see a terribly messy front room and kitchen. I began getting after all the children in sight, when Aaron spoke up.

"Well, don't just look at it that way, Mom," he said. "Look at all the clean places there are. See—here's a clean place, and there's a clean place!"

Oh, Aaron, clean places are all round. All around. Why don't I see them more? I walk into a room and all I see is the sweater you left on the floor, and the backpack and the basketball, and the dirty glass and apple core decorating the lamp table. But over here is an area of carpet many yards wide on which there are no cracker crumbs, no dirty socks, no scratch paper from school, and no little piles of bottle caps. A large area of clear, clean carpet! And the piano is in reasonably good shape. The couch is all right. There are, in fact, lots more clean places than dirty places.

Why do I look at the apple core and not the wonderful seascape on the wall? Why do I look at your dirty fingernails and not your well-shampooed hair? That's a clean place.

Why do I look at the place where you fail and not all the places where you succeed? Why do I look at the place where you are rude and not all the places where you are charming and delightful? Why do I look at the place where you and I yell at each other instead of at all the places where we smile and hug. Those are good places.

Okay, Aaron. How about a bargain? You do everything you can to minimize the messy places, and I'll try very hard to look for the clean places. I promise. At least once a day I will find one mess, look past it and say, "Hey, look at *that* clean place!"

The other day John said, "One of the mysteries of life to me is how Heavenly Father made the sun without burning his hands."

I don't know, John. I really do not know. And aren't mysteries wonderful? Wouldn't life be boring without them? What if we knew everything there is to know? What if we could just open to the index of the ultimate encyclopedia and find a reference—"How God created the sun without burning his hands, page 9,546."

Maybe sometime we can know everything. But right now I don't want to. I love standing wide-eyed before the mysteries. I love knowing sort of but not exactly why a waterfall runs down instead of up—why all rainbows show the same colors in the same order—why it takes two cells instead of one to begin a human life—how a cut finger can heal itself until it's brand new—how a bush can push magic through a thin, green stem to produce a gorgeous red rose—what is the amazing stuff that wraps two lovers in ecstasy just to be in the same room with one another—how a newborn baby knows it's time to be born, time to breathe, time to eat.

I have a feeling that if we knew it all, everything would be written in indexes and nothing in poems. And I love poems. They celebrate the mysteries, the wonder, the amazement of everything that makes us breathe a little faster just to think about it. Like how did God create the sun without burning his hands? And how did your mind even come up with the question? And how did we manage to be together for you to ask it of me? And how did we manage to be at all?

While Emily was at camp we each contributed a page to a letter. Aaron drew a picture and wrote beneath it, "I love you."

I told him that was very nice and gave it back to him to sign.

When Emily called me on the phone she said, "That sure was a funny letter Aaron sent me. He didn't even say a thing."

"But he wrote 'I love you,' " I said.

"He crossed that part out," she replied.

Well, shame on you, Aaron! Shame on anyone who crosses out love. The world cannot afford to lose any of that precious stuff. I have seen love crossed out, and every time it's a sad, sad thing.

I have seen little children friends let turns on a swing come between them. They have gone home in tears and crossed out "I love you." Fortunately children can cross out their crossings out as fast as they can make a dish of ice cream disappear.

I have seen big people friends let money come between them. One has more than the other and thinks he's better— or one borrows from the other and doesn't pay back. They frown and leave and cross out love.

I have seen parent and child let a system of beliefs come between them. One knows he has all the answers and the other comes up with different answers. The relationship is strained, or destroyed. Love that had been written again and again over the years is crossed out.

And I have seen husband and wife let the daily demands of domestic living come between them. Romance and sharing and support get put further and further away because the floor has to be mopped and the work at the office requires another weekend, and the children leave Mother exhausted. Or other things come between them, and love—love that was written in poetry and promises—is crossed out.

People change—relationships change—but those changes, I think, can be accommodated if one remembers that whatever the picture, love is the most important part.

Don't cross that part out.

The other night Katy and I were getting ready to say her prayers. I said to her, "You

know, Katy, I don't believe that God is up there in the sky somewhere. I think God is just here— around us."

"Around us," Katy said thoughtfully. "Just like ring-around-the-rosies. And when God falls down, that's the end of the world!"

What a thought, Katy! Fall down! The source that brought us here, that sustains us here, fall down? Impossible.

As for the end of the world, that's something we do have to think about from time to time. People have been talking about it, predicting it for centuries. Maybe it'll happen. At least, maybe the end of what we call the world will move into the beginning of something else—like ice changes into water, like blossoms change to fruit, or like an egg changes to a chicken. Shell has to be destroyed in the hatching, but that's all right.

I don't want you to worry about it. Things begin and end all the time, or seem to. But scientists have discovered that nothing really ends. It just changes its form. The world may "end." We will "end." But don't let that fool you. Do everything you can to live forever. Do everything you can to help the planet and the human race to live forever. And then just trust.

Life—you—the world—in one way or another is going to just go on and on and on. Because God does not fall down. God continues the dance forever.

The other day Katy said to me, "Mom, I know what rainbows are."

"What are they?" I asked.

"I think rainbows are the truth," she said.